Genetic Algorithms Made Simple

A Beginner's Guide to Solving Optimization Problems

PUBLISHED BY: Gerardo Caracas

Copyright © 2024 All rights reserved.

Table of Contents

Introduction

In an era defined by rapid technological advancement and boundless streams of data, the quest for efficient, intelligent solutions to complex problems has never been more pressing. In fields ranging from logistics and supply chain management to cutting-edge biomedical research and autonomous systems, decision-makers face intricate challenges that defy traditional approaches. Problems grow larger and more intricate, constraints clash with ambitious objectives, and the simple, time-tested methods of the past often falter under the weight of modern complexity. It is within this challenging landscape that optimization algorithms, particularly those inspired by nature, have found their place. Among these, Genetic Algorithms (GAs) stand out as a powerful and versatile tool, capable of tackling a wide array of difficult, multi-dimensional problems.

This eBook delves into the world of Genetic Algorithms, unraveling what they are, how they work, and why they remain a cornerstone of optimization and artificial intelligence. As you progress through the chapters, you will gain not only a foundational understanding of GAs, but also an appreciation for the elegance and flexibility they bring to problem-solving. While they may have roots stretching back to the 1970s, GAs are far from outdated. They have evolved in tandem with the broader field of AI, proving their worth in optimization tasks where other methods stumble.

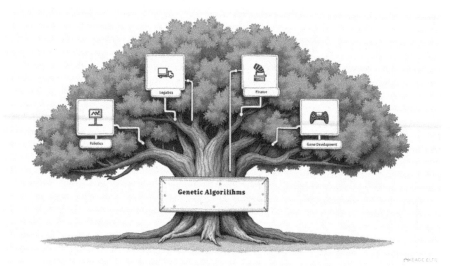

Figure 1 GA as a Central Solution for Multiple Domains

Before we dive into the mechanics, it's crucial to establish the "why." Why should you, as a student, practitioner, or enthusiast in the field of artificial intelligence, invest time and effort into understanding Genetic Algorithms? Why do these algorithms matter, and what makes them uniquely suited for certain classes of problems?

The Significance of Optimization

At their core, Genetic Algorithms are optimization tools, heuristic methods that iteratively search for better solutions to a given problem. To truly appreciate their importance, consider the ubiquitous nature of optimization. Every time a production line manager tries to shorten manufacturing times without compromising quality, they are tackling an optimization problem. When a shipping company seeks the shortest, most cost-effective routes to deliver goods across the globe, it engages in optimization. In machine learning, hyperparameter tuning, a critical step in building high-performing models, is essentially an optimization task, one that can be both time-consuming and non-trivial.

Optimization problems frequently resist simple, closed-form solutions. They can be:

- **Complex and Nonlinear:** Many real-world problems cannot be represented by neat equations. Instead, they span rugged "landscapes" of solutions with peaks and valleys that are difficult to navigate.

- **Multidimensional:** Tasks often involve juggling multiple variables and constraints simultaneously. Adjusting one parameter can cause ripple effects across an entire system.

- **Noisy and Uncertain:** Real-world data is rarely neat or perfect. Noise and uncertainty must be accounted for in seeking robust solutions.

- **Constrained by Time and Resources:** Solutions often need to be found quickly and efficiently, even when exhaustive approaches are impossible.

These conditions present significant challenges to conventional mathematical optimization techniques, and that's where Genetic Algorithms thrive. With their roots in natural selection and biological evolution, GAs provide a framework that inherently embraces complexity, nonlinearities, and uncertainty.

Figure 2 A Fitness Landscape

Nature as Inspiration

The power of GAs lies in their inspiration. Nature, over billions of years, has demonstrated a remarkable capacity to adapt, evolve, and overcome challenges. Genetic Algorithms borrow principles from evolutionary biology, natural selection, reproduction, and mutation, and apply them to computational problems. Instead of starting from a single guess and trying to improve it gradually, GAs maintain a population of candidate solutions. Each solution, akin to an organism, competes for survival based on its "fitness", a measure of how good the solution is at solving the problem.

Over successive generations, solutions "mate" through a process known as crossover, sharing their best traits in the hope of producing even fitter offspring. Random mutations ensure diversity and prevent the algorithm from stagnating on poor local optima. Gradually, through selection pressure and variation, the population evolves toward better and better solutions. This concept, mimicking the survival-of-the-fittest mechanism, enables GAs to tackle problems that are otherwise too complicated or too poorly understood to be solved by direct, analytical methods.

Consider tasks like designing a complex chemical compound with desired properties, optimizing neural network architectures without closed-form solutions, or scheduling tasks and resources in intricate workflows. In these domains, GAs thrive because they do not require gradients, derivatives, or perfect information. They only need a way to measure how "good" a solution is and a mechanism to evolve populations toward improvement.

Bridging the Gap Between Theory and Practice

One of the reasons GAs have retained their appeal is their versatility. They are not confined to a single domain or a particular type of problem. Practitioners in finance use Genetic Algorithms to balance portfolios and predict stock movements. Engineers employ GAs to fine-tune control parameters for drones, robots, and autonomous vehicles, making them more stable and efficient. Game developers harness their power to evolve non-player characters that adapt to players' strategies, providing engaging and unpredictable gameplay experiences.

For students and newcomers to AI, GAs offer a hands-on way to understand and experiment with optimization. They teach lessons that transcend the specific algorithm:

1. **Iterative Improvement:** The idea of starting with rough guesses and refining them iteratively can be applied to various AI and machine learning methods.

2. **Heuristics and Metaheuristics:** GAs are part of a broader class of heuristics, simple rules that help discover good solutions without guarantees of perfection. Understanding them opens doors to other advanced techniques like Particle Swarm Optimization (PSO) or Ant Colony Optimization (ACO).

3. **Balance Between Exploration and Exploitation:** GAs illustrate a core principle in optimization and machine learning. Too much exploitation (focusing on known

good solutions) can lead to stagnation, while too much exploration (random attempts) wastes resources. GAs find a healthy middle ground by evolving populations and retaining diversity.

As machine learning and AI mature, the line between model construction and model optimization often blurs. Techniques like Neural Architecture Search (NAS) rely on methods conceptually similar to GAs to find better neural network structures. Even if you never directly implement a Genetic Algorithm in a production setting, understanding their principles enhances your comprehension of a broad class of evolutionary and metaheuristic methods.

What to Expect in This eBook

This eBook is organized to guide you from fundamental principles to hands-on examples:

- **Chapter 1: What Are Genetic Algorithms?**
  Here, we lay the conceptual groundwork. You will learn about the origins of GAs, their key components, and the reasons they hold enduring importance.

- **Chapter 2: How GAs Mimic Natural Selection**
  Building on the introduction, we explore the biological metaphors at the heart of GAs. You will understand the processes of selection, crossover, and mutation in greater detail, and learn how these steps work together to evolve solutions.

- **Chapter 3: A Simple Example, Optimizing Task Scheduling**
  Finally, we bring theory to life with a concrete example. By tackling a straightforward scheduling problem, you'll see how GAs can be applied in a practical scenario. This example will help cement your understanding and provide a template for thinking about more complex problems.

By the end of this eBook, you will have a clear understanding of Genetic Algorithms, their place in the landscape of AI, and how to approach problems that might benefit from their unique strengths. You will also gain insights into the broader world of evolutionary computation and heuristics, equipping you with tools and concepts that can be applied across domains. Most importantly, you will develop an intuition for when and why to reach for a Genetic Algorithm, a skill that can prove invaluable as you navigate the complex terrain of optimization challenges.

As you turn the page and step into the world of Genetic Algorithms, keep in mind that these methods represent just one approach to optimization. Yet, their relevance and adaptability make them an essential part of any AI practitioner's toolkit. Whether you use them directly or simply appreciate their conceptual contributions, understanding GAs enhances your ability to tackle difficult, evolving problems, and that, in our increasingly complex world, is a skill well worth honing.

Chapter 1: What Are Genetic Algorithms?

This chapter introduces Genetic Algorithms (GAs), a class of optimization algorithms inspired by the principles of biological evolution. We begin by discussing the historical context and foundational concepts of GAs, exploring their core components, representation, selection, crossover, and mutation, and illustrating how these components mimic natural selection. We then examine why GAs are critical tools in modern optimization, highlighting their versatility and suitability for solving complex, high-dimensional problems. Finally, we review their importance in artificial intelligence and machine learning, demonstrating that an understanding of GAs provides valuable insights into heuristic problem-solving strategies and iterative improvement techniques.

1.1 Introduction

Genetic Algorithms (GAs) are search and optimization techniques that draw inspiration from the processes of evolution and natural selection. First conceptualized in the 1970s by John Holland and his colleagues, GAs were developed to address the limitations of traditional optimization methods, particularly when dealing with complex, non-linear, and high-dimensional search spaces. In many real-world scenarios, such as manufacturing scheduling, network routing, portfolio optimization, robotic path planning, and game strategy, finding an optimal solution can prove exceedingly difficult using classical methods. The solution landscapes are often riddled with local optima, discontinuities, or poorly understood relationships between decision variables.

Unlike gradient-based methods that rely on calculus and require differentiability, GAs operate on populations of candidate solutions, refining them iteratively using biologically inspired operators. The "fitness" of solutions dictates their reproductive success, ensuring that over generations, the population evolves toward more optimal configurations. The result is a robust, domain-agnostic tool capable of tackling problems that are otherwise intractable.

As we journey through this chapter, we will dissect the conceptual underpinnings of GAs, explore their key components, and discuss why they remain relevant in the modern landscape of artificial intelligence (AI) and machine learning (ML). Although GAs are not a panacea for all optimization problems, understanding them provides crucial insights into evolutionary computation, a field that continues to inspire innovative problem-solving approaches.

1.2 Historical Context and Biological Inspiration

The conceptual foundation of Genetic Algorithms derives from Darwinian principles of evolution: the notion that the fittest individuals are more likely to survive and pass on their genes to subsequent generations. In biology, organisms adapt to their environments over time, accumulating advantageous traits that enhance their chances of survival and reproduction. This simple yet powerful concept of "survival of the fittest" is at the heart of GAs.

John Holland's Influence:

John Holland at the University of Michigan was a pioneer in formalizing these ideas computationally. Holland's 1975 book, *Adaptation in Natural and Artificial Systems*, laid out a framework for applying evolutionary processes to problem-solving. His work set the stage for subsequent research that extended the use of evolutionary principles to a variety of domains.

Representation of Solutions as Chromosomes:

In a GA, candidate solutions to a given problem are often represented as strings called "chromosomes." These chromosomes can be binary strings, arrays of real numbers, or more complex data structures. The choice of representation depends on the problem's nature. For example, in a combinatorial optimization problem (like the Traveling Salesman Problem), a chromosome might be a permutation of city visits. In a parameter optimization problem, it might be a list of floating-point values representing design variables.

By coding solutions as chromosomes, GAs become a direct analogy to biological genes and chromosomes. Just as biological chromosomes carry genetic information that determines an organism's traits, GA chromosomes encode parameters that determine a solution's performance on a given problem.

1.3 Core Components of a Genetic Algorithm

A Genetic Algorithm typically involves a cycle of operations that guide a population of candidate solutions toward improvement over several iterations, commonly referred to as "generations." Although implementations can vary, most GAs include these fundamental steps:

1. **Initialization:**

   The initial population is usually generated randomly or via heuristics. Each member of the population (each chromosome) is a candidate solution. The diversity in this initial set helps ensure that the GA explores a wide swath of the search space.

2. **Fitness Evaluation:**

Each chromosome is evaluated using a fitness function, an objective function that quantifies how well that solution performs. The fitness function is problem-specific. For instance, in a portfolio optimization problem, the fitness might be a combination of high return and low risk. In a routing problem, the fitness might measure travel time or cost.

3. **Selection:**

The selection process identifies which chromosomes get to reproduce. Several selection strategies exist, such as roulette-wheel selection, tournament selection, and rank-based selection. The goal is to probabilistically favor better solutions while still maintaining some level of diversity. This ensures that more optimal individuals have a higher chance of passing their genes to the next generation, while less optimal individuals have a decreasing but nonzero probability of contributing.

4. **Crossover (Recombination):**

Inspired by sexual reproduction, crossover takes two parent chromosomes and combines their genetic material to form offspring. For example, if chromosomes are binary strings, a single-point crossover might split each parent's string at the same position and then swap the tails. More sophisticated crossover techniques can handle arrays of numbers or combinatorial structures. The key purpose of crossover is to exploit existing traits, allowing beneficial building blocks to recombine and produce even fitter offspring.

5. **Mutation:**

Mutation introduces random changes to chromosomes, representing the random genetic drift that occurs in natural populations. In binary representation, mutation could flip a bit. In numeric representations, mutation might perturb a value by a small random amount. Mutation's role is to prevent premature convergence, maintaining genetic diversity and ensuring that the GA can escape local optima.

6. **Replacement:**

After generating a new set of offspring, the GA must decide which individuals form the next generation. This can be done by replacing the entire parent population or using elitist strategies that preserve the best individuals. Replacement strategies balance exploration (introducing new genetic variants) and exploitation (retaining top-performing solutions).

7. **Termination:**

The GA runs for a fixed number of generations or until a convergence criterion is met. This might be when the population's fitness no longer improves or when an acceptable solution quality has been reached.

By iterating through these steps, GAs mimic evolutionary pressure, enabling solutions to evolve over time toward increased fitness.

1.4 Why Are Genetic Algorithms Important?

Versatility Across Domains:

Genetic Algorithms are problem-agnostic. They do not require domain-specific knowledge, differentiability, or continuity in the objective function. As a result, GAs can be applied to a wide range of fields including engineering design, finance, robotics, logistics, pharmaceuticals, and even creative domains like art and music generation. For instance, a GA can be used to schedule complex manufacturing tasks, optimize energy distribution in a smart grid, or evolve neural network architectures without needing closed-form gradients.

Handling Complexity and High-Dimensionality:

Many optimization problems today involve large search spaces and complex interactions among variables. Traditional methods, like gradient descent, linear programming, or exhaustive search, may fail to find good solutions efficiently. GAs, by sampling multiple points in the search space and stochastically evolving them, can handle these complexities more gracefully. They are particularly adept at escaping local minima because they maintain a diverse population rather than converging too rapidly to a single candidate solution.

No Gradient Needed:

One of the key advantages of GAs is that they do not rely on gradients, derivatives, or smoothness assumptions about the objective function. This stands in contrast to methods like gradient-based optimization or backpropagation in neural networks. If the objective function is non-differentiable, noisy, discontinuous, or only available as a "black-box" simulator, GAs remain usable. This makes them suitable for real-world problems where analytical gradients are unavailable, or the relationship between inputs and outputs is poorly understood.

Fostering Creativity and Innovation:

Because GAs are inherently exploratory and stochastic, they often yield novel, unexpected solutions. This creative aspect can be leveraged in engineering design to discover unconventional structures or materials. In games, GAs can evolve novel strategies or behaviors, sometimes resulting in solutions that human designers may not have envisioned. This innovation is not guaranteed, but the potential for serendipitous discoveries is an appealing feature of evolutionary algorithms.

1.5 Key Algorithmic Variants and Specialized Techniques

Over the years, researchers have developed many variants and hybrid approaches to GAs, each fine-tuned for specific problem characteristics:

- **Steady-State GAs:** Instead of replacing the entire population each generation, these algorithms replace only a few individuals at a time. This can slow convergence, potentially preserving diversity.

- **Elitism:** Ensures the best solutions from one generation carry over unchanged to the next, preserving top performers and often improving convergence speed.

- **Hybrid Genetic Algorithms:** Combine GAs with local search methods (e.g., hill climbing or simulated annealing) to fine-tune solutions within a generation. These hybrids, known as memetic algorithms, often achieve better performance by exploiting both global exploration (via GAs) and local exploitation (via local search).

- **Constraint Handling Techniques:** When dealing with constrained optimization problems, specialized operators, penalty functions, or repair methods ensure that generated solutions remain feasible.

- **Parallel and Distributed GAs:** Distributing populations across multiple processors or networks can greatly accelerate the search, as multiple candidate solutions can be evaluated and evolved in parallel. Such strategies are useful in large-scale industrial applications and complex simulations.

These and other refinements underscore the adaptability of GAs, which can be tailored to tackle a wide variety of problem types and computational environments.

1.6 Applications of Genetic Algorithms

Genetic Algorithms have been successfully applied to numerous domains. Their flexibility and robustness make them a popular choice in both academic research and industry.

Engineering and Design Optimization:

GAs help automate the design of complex systems. For example, in aerospace engineering, GAs can optimize wing shapes to reduce drag and improve fuel efficiency. In automotive engineering, they can help find parameters that reduce emissions or increase engine performance. Similarly, GAs are used in structural design, material selection, and product configuration tasks.

Robotics and Control:

In robotics, GAs can optimize control parameters for robot arms, legged robots, or autonomous drones. By evolving the control signals that lead to stable and efficient movement, engineers can discover motion patterns that are both robust and adaptive to changing environmental conditions.

Finance and Economics:

Portfolio optimization, trading strategy development, and risk management are areas where GAs find utility. For instance, GAs can explore large sets of potential asset combinations, adjusting allocations to maximize return while minimizing risk, even when the underlying objective functions are not smooth or easily differentiable.

Scheduling and Logistics:

In supply chain management, scheduling, and logistics, GAs can find efficient routing solutions that traditional algorithms struggle to handle. They can determine sequences of deliveries, transportation routes, or production schedules that minimize costs and meet stringent deadlines.

Machine Learning and AI:

While GAs are not as widely used as gradient-based methods for training neural networks, they can optimize neural architecture, hyperparameters, or feature sets.

Moreover, GAs can evolve rule sets, decision trees, or agent strategies in reinforcement learning contexts. By doing so, they circumvent the need for gradient information and potentially discover architectures that might be overlooked by more conventional approaches.

1.7 GAs in the Modern AI Landscape

Despite the rise of deep learning and gradient-based optimization techniques, Genetic Algorithms maintain a niche in the AI ecosystem. They are particularly valuable when:

- **Analytical Gradients Are Unavailable:** If the environment or simulation is too complex to derive gradients, GAs step in as a suitable alternative.

- **Exploration of Novel Solutions Is Desired:** When inventing creative solutions or strategies, GAs can wander into uncharted territories of the search space, uncovering designs or methods that deterministic approaches might never consider.

- **Robustness and Flexibility Matter:** GAs can adapt to changing problem requirements and can be integrated with other optimization methods. This adaptability makes them a good choice for dynamic environments.

Moreover, for AI beginners, learning about GAs provides exposure to evolutionary computation and heuristic optimization principles. Understanding these concepts fosters an appreciation for iterative improvement processes and the art of balancing exploration and exploitation, key themes in many advanced AI algorithms.

1.8 Educational Value for AI Beginners

For newcomers to AI and machine learning, Genetic Algorithms serve as a gentle introduction to optimization concepts without the mathematical intensity of calculus-based methods. By studying GAs, students learn the following core ideas:

- **Iterative Improvement:**

  Rather than attempting to solve a problem directly, GAs gradually improve upon existing solutions, mirroring the trial-and-error nature of real-world problem solving.

- **Heuristic Methods and Metaheuristics:**

  GAs are categorized as metaheuristics because they provide a general framework to solve optimization problems, not a domain-specific formula. This teaches beginners that clever strategies often outperform brute force, especially in complex environments.

- **Diversity and Population-Based Methods:**

  By handling a population of solutions, GAs emphasize the importance of diversity. This encourages a more global perspective in problem-solving, wherein considering multiple candidate solutions can lead to a more robust final result.

- **Balance of Exploration and Exploitation:**

  GAs illustrate the delicate balance between searching for new solutions (exploration) and refining known good solutions (exploitation). Understanding this trade-off is essential not only in GAs but also in other AI methods, such as reinforcement learning and evolutionary strategies.

1.9 Conclusion

Genetic Algorithms represent a powerful class of optimization tools grounded in the principles of natural selection. By emulating evolutionary pressures, selection, reproduction, crossover, and mutation, GAs iteratively refine populations of candidate solutions. This process allows them to excel in complex, high-dimensional search spaces where traditional optimization methods falter.

Their versatility, independence from gradient information, and ability to discover novel solutions ensure GAs remain relevant today, even in an era dominated by deep learning and advanced AI frameworks. As we progress through this ebook, we will delve deeper into the theoretical foundations of GAs, examine case studies, and demonstrate how to implement them effectively for diverse real-world applications. Understanding Genetic Algorithms provides invaluable insights into the broader domain of evolutionary computation, offering lessons in heuristic problem-solving and the continuous pursuit of better solutions.

Chapter 2: How Genetic Algorithms Mimic Natural Selection

In this chapter, we delve deeper into the evolutionary underpinnings of Genetic Algorithms (GAs) and examine how these computational methods emulate the process of natural selection. By drawing analogies between biological evolution and algorithmic steps, initialization, selection, crossover, mutation, evaluation, and termination, we illustrate how GAs systematically search the solution space. We clarify how these steps interrelate, discuss diverse strategies and variations for each, and highlight the fundamental role of the fitness function in guiding the evolutionary process. This chapter establishes a more thorough conceptual understanding of how GAs work, setting the stage for more advanced techniques and applications in subsequent chapters.

2.1 Introduction

Genetic Algorithms are not merely inspired by evolution on a superficial level; they incorporate key principles of Darwinian theory into their operational paradigm. In nature, species evolve through the differential survival and reproduction of individuals with advantageous traits, leading to the gradual accumulation of beneficial genetic material over many generations. GAs harness this core idea, applying it to computational problem-solving by continuously improving populations of candidate solutions.

The essential workflow of a GA closely resembles biological evolution. Initially, a population of potential solutions is created, analogous to a population of organisms. Through processes like selection, crossover, and mutation, the GA refines these solutions over multiple generations. This iterative cycle continues until a termination condition is met, such as finding a solution that meets desired quality standards or reaching a predetermined computational limit.

In this chapter, we map the fundamental steps of a GA, Initialization, Selection, Crossover, Mutation, Evaluation, and Termination, back to the central concepts of natural selection and evolutionary biology. Through a more comprehensive exploration of these steps, readers will gain a deeper appreciation for how GAs "evolve" solutions to complex optimization problems.

2.2 Natural Selection in the Biological World

To understand how GAs mimic natural selection, it is helpful to briefly revisit Darwin's theory of evolution by means of natural selection. In the biological world:

1. **Variation:**

   Within any given species, individuals exhibit differences in traits, be it physical attributes, behavioral tendencies, or genetic markers. This variation often arises from natural genetic recombination and occasional mutations in the DNA.

2. **Inheritance:**

Traits are passed from one generation to the next through genetic material. Offspring inherit characteristics from their parents, forming a genetic link that transmits advantageous traits forward in time.

3. **Selection Pressure:**

Not all individuals survive or reproduce equally. Environmental factors, such as availability of food, presence of predators, or climatic conditions, exert "selection pressure." Individuals best adapted to the current environment have a higher probability of survival and reproduction.

4. **Gradual Change over Generations:**

Over many generations, these processes lead to a gradual increase in the prevalence of advantageous traits. Eventually, this can result in the emergence of new species or the refinement of a species' characteristics to fit its ecological niche more effectively.

GAs encapsulate these principles in a digital environment, where candidate solutions act as "organisms," problem constraints form the "environment," and the notion of "fitness" simulates how well an individual solution aligns with the objectives at hand.

2.3 Initialization: Seeding the Digital Gene Pool

Biological Parallel:

In nature, any given species starts with a wide range of genetic variation. Genetic differences come from historical mutations, gene flow, and recombination events over many generations. Although no single generation starts "from scratch," the principle of variation at the start of a GA's execution aligns with the variation observed in biological populations.

GA Implementation:

Initialization sets the stage for the evolutionary search. GAs typically begin with a randomly generated population of candidate solutions. Each member of this population, often represented as a chromosome-like structure, encodes a set of parameters or variables relevant to the optimization problem. The size of this population depends on computational resources and problem complexity, but it must be large enough to explore a meaningful swath of the solution space.

Strategic Considerations:

- **Random Initialization:** Most commonly, solutions are assigned random values within predefined bounds. For instance, if optimizing the dimensions of a machine component, each dimension might be a random real number within the feasible range.

- **Heuristic or Informed Initialization:** In some cases, partial domain knowledge can guide initial solution guesses. If a known feasible solution exists, starting the population around that point may accelerate convergence.

- **Maintaining Diversity:** Initialization strategies that ensure a broad spread of candidate solutions can prevent premature convergence and improve the algorithm's chances of finding global optima.

By carefully choosing the initial population, GA practitioners set the evolutionary process on a path that encourages broad exploration, just as a varied gene pool supports a species' adaptability in nature.

2.4 Selection: Choosing the Fittest Individuals

Biological Parallel:

In the wild, environmental conditions favor certain traits. Faster antelopes evade predators more effectively, stronger predators secure more prey, and well-camouflaged insects avoid detection. Those individuals with advantageous traits tend to survive longer and produce more offspring. Over successive generations, these beneficial traits become more common within the population.

GA Implementation:

Selection mechanisms in GAs choose which individuals get to "reproduce," i.e., which solutions pass their encoded traits into the next generation. Typically, this is done probabilistically, with better solutions, those that achieve higher fitness scores, enjoying a higher probability of selection.

Common Selection Methods:

- **Roulette-Wheel Selection:** Individuals are selected with a probability proportional to their fitness. Imagine a roulette wheel where each individual occupies a segment sized by its fitness value. Spinning the wheel multiple times picks individuals to form the mating pool.

- **Tournament Selection:** A small subset of individuals is picked at random, and the best among them is chosen for reproduction. This method balances selection pressure and computational efficiency.

- **Rank-Based Selection:** Instead of using raw fitness values directly, individuals are ranked by fitness. Selection probability is assigned based on the rank. This method avoids issues where a few highly fit individuals dominate the population.

- **Elitism:** Ensures that the best individual(s) from one generation carry over unchanged to the next, guaranteeing that progress is not lost.

By applying these selection methods, GAs emulate natural selection's focus on "survival of the fittest" while still maintaining genetic diversity. The result is a dynamic system that gradually biases the population toward regions of higher fitness, but without completely eliminating genetic variety.

2.5 Crossover (Reproduction): Combining Genetic Material

Biological Parallel:

Reproduction in biology involves the combination of genetic information from two parents. In sexual reproduction, offspring inherit a mix of traits from both their mother and father. This recombination ensures that beneficial traits can spread through the population, mixing and matching genetic material in novel ways.

GA Implementation:

In a GA, crossover (often called recombination) combines parts of two parent solutions to produce offspring solutions. The specific crossover operator depends on the representation of the solution:

- **Binary Representation:** If the chromosome is a binary string, a single-point crossover might split the parents' strings at a chosen position and exchange the segments after that point.

- **Real-Valued Representation:** If the chromosome is a vector of floating-point parameters, arithmetic crossover can create offspring by taking weighted averages of corresponding parameters.

- **Permutation Representation:** For combinatorial problems like routing or scheduling, specialized crossover operators ensure that offspring remain feasible permutations.

Role of Crossover:

Crossover operators play a critical role in enabling the transfer of "building blocks" of good solutions from one generation to the next. By mixing traits, GAs can produce solutions that inherit strengths from multiple parents. This process accelerates the search for optimal or near-optimal solutions, reflecting how sexual reproduction in nature generates offspring with potentially advantageous combinations of traits.

2.6 Mutation: Introducing Random Variation

Biological Parallel:

Mutation in biology occurs when errors in DNA replication or external factors (radiation, chemicals, viruses) alter an organism's genetic sequence. Most mutations are neutral or deleterious, but occasionally a mutation can provide a beneficial trait. Over time, these rare beneficial mutations can significantly influence a species' evolution.

GA Implementation:

In GAs, mutation serves a critical role in maintaining diversity within the population. Without mutation, the GA might converge too quickly to a local optimum, losing the ability to explore new regions of the search space.

Mutation Operators:

- **Bit-Flip Mutation:** For binary strings, flipping a bit from 0 to 1 or vice versa introduces small genetic changes.

- **Gaussian Perturbation:** For real-valued parameters, adding a small random perturbation (drawn from a normal distribution) can nudge solutions into new territory.

- **Swap or Inversion Mutation:** In permutation-based problems, randomly swapping two elements or reversing a substring can explore different permutations.

Mutation Rate Considerations:

The mutation rate is a crucial parameter. A too-high mutation rate disrupts the genetic information and reduces the GA to a random search. A too-low mutation rate risks stagnation. Balancing mutation levels ensures sustained exploration and the ongoing potential to escape from local optima.

2.7 Evaluation: Measuring Fitness to Guide Evolution

Biological Parallel:

In nature, "fitness" is the measure of an organism's success at surviving and reproducing in its environment. There is no explicit numeric fitness score in the wild, but differential survival rates and reproductive success effectively encode a fitness function favoring certain traits.

GA Implementation:

In a GA, fitness is quantified using a fitness function (or objective function) that reflects the quality of a solution. This is a critical concept: the fitness function translates problem-specific goals into a measurable metric that the GA can use to rank and compare solutions.

Designing a Fitness Function:

- **Validity and Constraints:** The fitness function must guide solutions toward feasibility. For constrained optimization, infeasible solutions can be penalized.

- **Scaling and Normalization:** Sometimes raw objective values require scaling for effective selection. For example, if the objective function values differ by many orders of magnitude, normalizing the fitness values can help maintain a stable search process.

- **Multiple Objectives:** In problems with multiple competing criteria (e.g., cost vs. quality), multi-objective fitness functions or Pareto-based evaluations can be employed.

The fitness function drives the evolutionary engine of the GA. By associating each solution with a measurable outcome, the algorithm "knows" which individuals are worth reproducing and which should be discarded.

2.8 Termination: Knowing When to Stop

Biological Parallel:

Biological evolution does not have a predetermined stopping point; it continues indefinitely as environments change and new challenges arise. In computation, however, resources are finite, and optimization problems typically have practical endpoints.

GA Implementation:

A GA must have criteria for termination. Common stopping conditions include:

- **Fixed Number of Generations:** Run the GA for a predetermined number of generations and then halt, returning the best solution found so far.

- **Fitness Threshold:** Stop when a solution with fitness above a certain threshold is discovered, indicating that the problem's requirements are met.

- **Convergence Criteria:** Monitor improvements in the best fitness value over recent generations. If no significant improvement occurs for several generations, the algorithm may have converged.

- **Time or Resource Limit:** Limit the running time or computational cost. When resources are exhausted, return the current best solution.

Choosing termination criteria involves balancing the desire for better solutions against the computational cost. In practice, setting multiple termination conditions can provide both efficiency and reasonable assurance of solution quality.

2.9 Integrating the Steps into a Cohesive Evolutionary Cycle

While we have discussed each GA step individually, their true power lies in their integration into an iterative, evolutionary cycle:

1. **Initialize:** Start with a diverse population.

2. **Evaluate:** Compute the fitness of each solution.

3. **Select:** Choose the best individuals to form a mating pool.

4. **Crossover & Mutate:** Create offspring with new genetic combinations and variations.

5. **Evaluate (Again):** Measure the new generation's fitness.

6. **Replace:** Form the next generation by retaining strong solutions and discarding weaker ones.

7. **Check Termination:** If conditions are met, stop. Otherwise, repeat the cycle.

Over time, this cycle shifts the population's "genetic makeup" toward regions of higher fitness. Like natural selection, GAs leverage variation, heredity, and selection pressure to evolve superior solutions.

2.10 Variations and Adaptations in GA Operators

Real-world GA implementations often refine or alter the fundamental operators:

- **Adaptive Mutation Rates:** Mutation rates can be adjusted dynamically based on convergence metrics. Higher mutation rates might be applied when the population's diversity decreases.

- **Niche and Speciation Methods:** Inspired by biodiversity in nature, niche techniques ensure that multiple promising regions of the search space are explored simultaneously.

- **Hybridized Approaches:** Combining GAs with local search methods, simulated annealing, or other heuristic optimization approaches can produce more efficient or accurate results.

- **Advanced Selection Schemes:** Using advanced selection strategies can fine-tune the balance between exploration and exploitation.

These variations demonstrate that GAs are not static methods. Much like biological evolution, they adapt, evolve, and improve through experimentation and innovation.

2.11 Summary and Insights

Genetic Algorithms mirror natural selection in a computational setting, using an iterative process of selection, reproduction, and mutation to evolve solutions that are well-suited to their defined environment (the problem space). By carefully designing fitness functions, initialization strategies, selection operators, crossover mechanisms, and mutation rates, engineers and data scientists can channel the principles of biological evolution into powerful optimization tools.

Through the steps examined in this chapter, we see that GAs are more than random search algorithms: they are guided by the metaphor of evolution, harnessing structured variation and selective pressure to navigate complex landscapes. Understanding this cvolutionary analogy is key for leveraging GAs effectively and interpreting their results with nuance.

Chapter 3: A Simple Example - Optimizing Task Scheduling

In this chapter, we will transition from theory to practice by implementing a Genetic Algorithm (GA) in Python 3.5. We will demonstrate how to set up a GA to optimize a simple task-scheduling problem, arranging a set of tasks to minimize total completion time while prioritizing important tasks. This hands-on example will solidify concepts introduced in previous chapters and illustrate how to translate GA design decisions into functioning code. By the end of this chapter, you will have a working GA implementation for a scheduling problem and understand how to adapt the code for other optimization tasks.

3.1 Problem Setup

Our sample problem involves scheduling a set of tasks, each with a certain duration and priority. The tasks must be arranged in an order that minimizes a fitness function emphasizing both efficiency and priority. High-priority tasks should appear earlier in the schedule, reducing their weighted completion time.

Tasks:

- Math Homework: 2 hours, priority 1 (high)

- English Essay: 3 hours, priority 2

- Science Project: 4 hours, priority 1 (high)

- History Reading: 2 hours, priority 3

- Art Practice: 1 hour, priority 4

We assume all tasks must be completed. The goal is to minimize a fitness score that rewards having high-priority tasks completed sooner.

Fitness Function Consideration:

Since all tasks will be completed, the total number of hours is fixed (2 + 3 + 4 + 2 + 1 = 12 hours). However, the order matters. Let's define the fitness as the sum over all tasks of (cumulative completion time * task priority). Placing high-priority tasks earlier reduces their weighted completion time, thereby reducing the overall fitness.

For each candidate schedule (an ordering of tasks):

1. Initialize `cumulative_time = 0` and `fitness = 0`.

2. For each task in order:

- o Add the task's hours to `cumulative_time`.

- o Add `cumulative_time * task_priority` to `fitness`.

A lower fitness value is better, as it indicates high-priority tasks are being completed earlier.

3.2 Representing the Population

Individual Representation:

Each individual is a permutation of the tasks. For example, a valid individual could be represented as a list of tasks:

```
individual = [
    ("Math Homework", 2, 1),
    ("English Essay", 3, 2),
    ("Science Project", 4, 1),
    ("History Reading", 2, 3),
    ("Art Practice", 1, 4)
]
```

Any permutation of these five tasks is a distinct schedule (individual).

Initial Population Generation:

We will create an initial population by randomly shuffling the list of tasks multiple times. This ensures diversity at the start.

3.3 Evaluating Fitness

The fitness function will calculate the weighted completion time as described. Here is a code snippet for the fitness function:

```
def calculate_fitness(individual):
    cumulative_time = 0
    fitness = 0
    for task in individual:
        duration = task[1]
        priority = task[2]
        cumulative_time += duration
        # Weighted completion time:
        fitness += cumulative_time * priority
    return fitness
```

This function ensures that schedules penalizing high-priority tasks placed later in the order result in higher fitness values.

3.4 Selection Mechanisms

For simplicity, we will use **tournament selection**:

1. Randomly choose a few individuals from the population.

2. Select the best (lowest fitness) individual from that subset.

This gives fitter individuals a higher chance to reproduce without overly restricting genetic diversity.

```python
import random

def tournament_selection(population, fitnesses, k=3):
    # k is tournament size
    selected = random.sample(list(zip(population, fitnesses)), k)
    selected.sort(key=lambda x: x[1])   # sort by fitness (lower is better)
    return selected[0][0]   # return the individual with the best (lowest)
fitness
```

3.5 Crossover Operators

To combine genetic material from two parents, we will use a **partially matched crossover (PMX)** or a simple ordered crossover method that ensures no tasks are duplicated and all tasks appear exactly once in the child.

For simplicity, we'll demonstrate a straightforward ordered crossover:

```python
def crossover(parent1, parent2):
    # Ordered crossover
    size = len(parent1)
    start, end = sorted([random.randint(0, size - 1) for _ in range(2)])

    child = [None] * size
    # Copy a slice from parent1
    child[start:end + 1] = parent1[start:end + 1]

    # Fill the remaining positions with the tasks from parent2 in order
    # that are not already in the child
    p2_items = [task for task in parent2 if task not in child]

    idx = 0
    for i in range(size):
        if child[i] is None:
            child[i] = p2_items[idx]
            idx += 1

    return child
```

This ensures a child inherits a segment from one parent and the rest from the other, maintaining a valid permutation of tasks.

3.6 Mutation Operators

We will implement a simple swap mutation: pick two positions in the individual and swap them. This introduces variety and helps the GA escape local optima.

```python
def mutate(individual, mutation_rate=0.1):
    new_ind = individual[:]
    if random.random() < mutation_rate:
        i, j = random.sample(range(len(individual)), 2)
        new_ind[i], new_ind[j] = new_ind[j], new_ind[i]
    return new_ind
```

A small mutation rate (e.g., 10%) is often effective. Adjusting this rate may improve results depending on the problem's complexity.

3.7 The Evolutionary Cycle

The GA proceeds in generations:

1. **Initialization:** Randomly generate an initial population.

2. **Evaluation:** Calculate fitness for all individuals.

3. **Selection and Reproduction:** Use selection to pick parents, then apply crossover and mutation to create offspring.

4. **Replacement:** Form the new generation from the offspring (and possibly some elites).

5. **Termination:** Stop after a fixed number of generations or when no improvement is observed for several generations.

For demonstration, we'll run the GA for a fixed number of generations.

3.8 Full Example Code

Below is the complete Python 3.5 code implementing the GA described above. You can copy and paste this into a .py file and run it. Make sure you have Python 3.5 or newer installed.

```python
import random

# Tasks: (Name, Duration, Priority)
TASKS = [
```

```
        ("Math Homework", 2, 1),
        ("English Essay", 3, 2),
        ("Science Project", 4, 1),
        ("History Reading", 2, 3),
        ("Art Practice", 1, 4)
]


def calculate_fitness(individual):
    cumulative_time = 0
    fitness = 0
    for task in individual:
        duration = task[1]
        priority = task[2]
        cumulative_time += duration
        fitness += cumulative_time * priority
    return fitness


def tournament_selection(population, fitnesses, k=3):
    selected = random.sample(list(zip(population, fitnesses)), k)
    selected.sort(key=lambda x: x[1])
    return selected[0][0]


def crossover(parent1, parent2):
    size = len(parent1)
    start, end = sorted([random.randint(0, size - 1) for _ in range(2)])

    child = [None] * size
    # Copy a slice from parent1
    child[start:end + 1] = parent1[start:end + 1]

    # Fill remaining with parent2's tasks not in child
    p2_items = [task for task in parent2 if task not in child]

    idx = 0
    for i in range(size):
        if child[i] is None:
            child[i] = p2_items[idx]
            idx += 1
    return child


def mutate(individual, mutation_rate=0.1):
    new_ind = individual[:]
    if random.random() < mutation_rate:
        i, j = random.sample(range(len(individual)), 2)
        new_ind[i], new_ind[j] = new_ind[j], new_ind[i]
    return new_ind


def create_initial_population(pop_size=20):
    population = []
    for _ in range(pop_size):
        ind = TASKS[:]
        random.shuffle(ind)
```

```python
            population.append(ind)
        return population


def run_ga(generations=50, pop_size=20, mutation_rate=0.1):
    # Initialize population
    population = create_initial_population(pop_size)

    for gen in range(generations):
        # Evaluate fitness
        fitnesses = [calculate_fitness(ind) for ind in population]

        # Track best
        best_fitness = min(fitnesses)
        best_individual = population[fitnesses.index(best_fitness)]

        # Print progress
        print("Generation:", gen, "Best Fitness:", best_fitness)

        # Create new population
        new_population = []

        # We can implement elitism by saving the best one
        new_population.append(best_individual)

        # Produce offspring
        while len(new_population) < pop_size:
            parent1 = tournament_selection(population, fitnesses)
            parent2 = tournament_selection(population, fitnesses)
            child = crossover(parent1, parent2)
            child = mutate(child, mutation_rate)
            new_population.append(child)

        population = new_population

    # After last generation, return the best solution found
    final_fitnesses = [calculate_fitness(ind) for ind in population]
    best_final_fitness = min(final_fitnesses)
    best_final_ind = population[final_fitnesses.index(best_final_fitness)]
    return best_final_ind, best_final_fitness


if __name__ == "__main__":
    best_schedule, best_score = run_ga(generations=100, pop_size=30,
mutation_rate=0.1)
    print("\nBest schedule found:")
    for i, task in enumerate(best_schedule):
        print(i + 1, "->", task[0], "(Duration:", task[1], "Priority:",
task[2], ")")
    print("Final Fitness Score:", best_score)
```

3.9 Interpreting the Results

After running the code, the GA will report improvements in the best fitness score from generation to generation. Eventually, it should identify an ordering of tasks that places high-priority tasks earlier, resulting in a relatively low fitness score.

For instance, a good final schedule might begin with the high-priority tasks (Math Homework and Science Project) so their contribution to the cumulative weighted completion time is minimized.

3.10 Extending the Example

The techniques shown here are easily adaptable. You can:

- Add more tasks or different constraints.

- Adjust the fitness function to include different priorities or even skipping low-priority tasks if allowed.

- Change the selection, crossover, or mutation methods to see if the GA converges faster.

- Use different termination criteria, such as stopping when no improvement occurs after a certain number of generations.

This simple scheduling example provides a foundation for applying GAs to more complex optimization tasks. By understanding the code and concepts presented here, you are now equipped to experiment, refine, and extend the GA approach to suit your own problem domains.

Conclusion

Over the course of this eBook, we have journeyed through the conceptual foundations, biological inspirations, core components, and a practical implementation of Genetic Algorithms (GAs). Beginning with a high-level overview of why optimization is a critical concern in today's data-driven world, we explored how GAs fit into the broader context of artificial intelligence and machine learning. Through theory and practice, we have seen firsthand that GAs are far more than a historical curiosity; they remain a viable and often transformative approach to solving complex optimization problems.

Reflecting on Key Concepts

In the first chapter, we established what Genetic Algorithms are and why they matter. We positioned them as powerful heuristic search methods inspired by the principles of natural selection, fundamental processes that have led to the immense diversity of life on Earth. By encoding candidate solutions as chromosomes and iterating through generations of selection, crossover, and mutation, GAs effectively "evolve" solutions. Unlike many classical optimization techniques, GAs do not rely on gradient information, making them ideal for problems where analytical solutions are unknown or infeasible. This flexibility is part of their enduring relevance.

In the second chapter, we delved deeper into the biological analogy. We examined how key GA operations mirror evolutionary mechanisms: random initialization ensures genetic diversity, selection mimics survival of the fittest, crossover recombines genetic material from parents, and mutation introduces the variability needed to explore uncharted solution spaces. Importantly, we discussed how the fitness function serves as the ultimate arbiter of success, guiding the GA's search through a complex, multidimensional landscape of possible solutions. Understanding these steps allows practitioners to configure and fine-tune GAs for their specific domains, be it portfolio optimization, supply chain management, or the design of advanced engineering systems.

The third chapter brought theory to life with a hands-on example. By implementing a GA in Python 3.5 to optimize a simple scheduling problem, we grounded abstract concepts in tangible code. Readers saw how to represent a population, measure fitness, select parents, produce offspring, and introduce mutations, all culminating in a working solution that improves over multiple generations. This practical demonstration bridges the gap between conceptual understanding and real-world applicability, illustrating how GAs can be rapidly prototyped, tested, and refined.

Core Insights and Lasting Value

One of the most valuable aspects of mastering Genetic Algorithms is not just the skill of using this particular tool, but the conceptual toolkit that comes with it. GAs impart important lessons that are broadly applicable to AI and optimization:

1. **Iterative Refinement:**

   GAs thrive under the paradigm of iterative improvement. Rather than expecting an immediate optimal solution, they refine populations over time, mirroring the adaptive, trial-and-error process that characterizes many complex real-world tasks.

2. **Balancing Exploration and Exploitation:**

   Central to GAs is the tension between searching widely for new opportunities (exploration) and honing in on promising regions of the solution space (exploitation). Mastering this balance is crucial in a wide range of optimization and learning methods, from reinforcement learning agents exploring new strategies to hyperparameter tuning in machine learning models.

3. **Versatility and Adaptability:**

GAs do not rely on domain-specific equations or gradient-based methods. Their only requirement is a well-defined fitness function. This domain-agnostic nature allows them to be applied in fields as varied as logistics, finance, robotics, creative design, and beyond. Moreover, many advanced optimization methods borrow ideas directly from evolutionary computation. Understanding GAs can ease the transition to studying more specialized evolutionary algorithms, metaheuristics, or hybrid models.

4. **Handling Complexity and Uncertainty:**

Modern optimization problems are rarely simple. They often involve numerous variables, constraints, noisy data, and non-linear interactions that elude straightforward analytical solutions. GAs, with their population-based approach and stochastic search capabilities, are well-suited to navigate these challenging landscapes. Even if a GA does not always yield a global optimum, it often finds sufficiently good solutions within reasonable time frames.

Looking Ahead

As the fields of machine learning, artificial intelligence, and computational optimization continue to evolve, the methods we rely on will undoubtedly shift and grow in complexity. Deep learning and gradient-based optimization have taken center stage in many AI applications, but GAs continue to hold their own niche, particularly in domains where gradients are unavailable, where creativity and exploration are paramount, or where hybrid approaches integrating multiple optimization techniques prove the most effective.

Learning Genetic Algorithms equips you with a valuable perspective: It reminds you that nature has solved countless optimization problems over billions of years through evolutionary processes, and that this principle can be harnessed, in a simplified computational form, to approach hard problems in inventive ways. Whether you end up deploying GAs directly in your projects or simply use their principles to inform your approach to problem-solving, the underlying lessons remain vital.

Conclusion

In sum, this eBook has introduced you to the rich conceptual framework and practical techniques behind Genetic Algorithms. We have explored the why, how, and when of GAs, from the broad significance of optimization to the intricacies of natural selection and evolutionary operators, culminating in a step-by-step coding example.

The understanding you have gained positions you to recognize when a GA may be the right tool for a given challenge. It also provides a foundation for further study, whether you choose to delve into advanced variants, integrate GAs with other heuristic or gradient-based methods, or explore entirely different evolutionary algorithms.

Armed with this knowledge, you can approach complex optimization problems with greater confidence and creativity. Genetic Algorithms are not a silver bullet, but they represent a powerful arrow in the quiver of anyone seeking robust, flexible, and often surprisingly elegant solutions to the toughest challenges in AI and beyond.

www.ingramcontent.com/pod-product-compliance
Lightning Source LLC
LaVergne TN
LVHW081807050326
832903LV00027B/2137